Red Ridir

retold by Stan Cullimore

LONGMAN

This is the story of a little girl
who was always as good as gold.
Her name was little Red Riding Hood
and she was only six years old!

One day her Mum made a brambly pie –
With a sweet and brambly smell!
"Take this to Gran," said Mum to the girl,
"Your Granny is *not* feeling well."

So the good little girl picked up the pie
and put on her red riding hood.
Then off she went to her Granny's house,
which was hidden away in a wood.

But as she happily walked through the trees,
somebody watched her go by...
A naughty wolf, with a hungry tummy
had a naughty look in his eye!

That hungry wolf, he looked at the girl
wearing her red riding hood.
He licked his lips and he rubbed his
	tummy –
and said, "I'd eat *her* if I could!"

So he ran through the trees to
	Granny's house
where he shouted, "Quick, let me in!"
But when Granny opened her little
	front door...
He popped her straight in the bin!

He ran through the house and jumped
   into bed
and snuggled up under the sheet –
and said to himself with a naughty smile
"That girl will be *lovely* to eat!"

When the good little girl got to
    Granny's house
the door was open wide...
So she put down the pie and wiped
    her feet,
and then she went inside.

She went through the house
    to Granny's room
and saw someone lying in bed.
But it didn't look quite like her Granny –
and so the little girl said,

"Oh, Granny – what hairy hands
    you have."
To which the Wolf replied...
"I know my hands are hairy, my child.
But come in and sit by my side."

"Oh, Granny – what beady eyes you have."

The Wolf, he smiled and said...

"My eyes are beady but I'm getting quite old.
Come closer and sit by my bed."

"Oh, Granny – what pointy teeth you have."

The Wolf, he got *mad* as can be...

"Just come here at once, you *stupid* child

I'm hungry and *you* are my tea!"

With a crash the door flew open wide,
and there was the smelly bin.
The lid flew off and Granny jumped out,
Red Riding Hood started to grin.

She ran at the Wolf – looking
ever so cross –
and **SPLATTED** the pie in his face.

splat!

The Wolf cried out, "I want my Mummy!"
and ran – right out of the place...

That was the last that ever was heard
of the naughty Wolf in the wood.
From that day on he changed his ways
because of Red Riding Hood...

and her Gran!

3 Fang Lane,
Bitem,
Sore.

Dear little Red Riding Hood.
(and Granny)

I'm sorry I was so
~~nort~~ ~~naut~~ naughty. I
have made you a present,
I hope you like it !

Yours

The Wolf
x x x x